Thammi's Gift

First published in India by HarperCollins Publishers 2022
Building No 10, Tower A, 4th Floor, DLF Cyber City, Phase II,
Gurugram – 122002

2 4 6 8 10 9 7 5 3 1

P-ISBN: 9789356293397
E-ISBN: 9789356293403

Cover, design & illustrations: Priya Kuriyan

Typeset in Adobe Garamond Pro – 17pt/25 by Priya Kuriyan

Printed and bound at Nutech Print Services - India

HarperCollinsIn

Thammi's Gift

Himani Dalmia

illustrated by

Priya Kuriyan

HarperCollinsChildren'sBooks

For Mahima Kaur, Dalbir Kaur Madan and Neil Jarial - who have kept the fire for stories burning in my children. And for librarians everywhere - who are silently nurturing the thinkers of tomorrow.

Himani

For Tara Mittra and all the kids who discover the pleasures of reading.

Priya

Devika had a library at home.

Her Thammi had been a librarian. She had created big, beautiful libraries in schools. And she had created a library for Devika at home as a present for her before she was even born.

She had bought hundreds of books of every kind. Books for babies, books for toddlers, books for older children. Books about bears, books about dragons, books about grandmas, books about trucks, books about magic.

ANIMATARIUM

Thammi had read to Devika while
she was still in her Mamma's belly...

she had read to Devika the day
she was born...

as she grew bigger and
reclined on her lap...

as she learned how to
sit and roll about...

...as she started to walk and talk.
Every few days, Thammi would come home laden with books and her vast home library grew and grew.

Then, one day, a few months after Devika's new baby sister arrived, Thammi stopped coming over.

"Thammi has become a star," her Mamma explained to her. Devika felt sad. She missed her Thammi. She wanted to snuggle into her grandma's lap and listen to stories.

Her Mamma, Daddy, Nana and Nanima still read to her and her sister. They would read in bed first thing on waking up even though Daddy grumbled, "It's too early!" They would read in between making puzzles or building with blocks or playing with their dinky cars. They would read before their afternoon naps. They would ask Daddy to read while they ate their meals, though he often refused and wanted to talk instead. They would read in the car. They would even read while sitting on the pot.

Some years later, when Devika was five years old, Mamma chose a bedtime book one night about a little girl and a blue kangaroo starting at a new school.

Devika was sad. She knew she would be starting big school on Monday. She did not want to go to a new school.

When she thought about her new school, she did not want to eat. She did not want to play with her animal guys. She felt angry with her little sister. She wanted to hold her Daddy and cry. She found it difficult to fall asleep. She woke up at night and lay awake in her Mamma's arms for a long time.

After listening to the story, Devika wondered which of her animal guys she would like to take to her new school. Perhaps the pony...

As Devika's mind wandered, sleep washed over her.

Devika woke up early on Friday morning. She ran to her room. The first light of dawn was emerging from behind the trees. There were still a few stars in the sky.

Suddenly, she saw one star becoming bigger. And bigger. And bigger. Until it became bigger than the sun and the moon! She watched, mesmerized, and, suddenly, the star shot towards her in spirals of light. Devika took a step back. The star bounced into her room and began to take the shape of a person!

Devika was scared at first. Was this a monster? Then she was excited. Could it be a fairy? And, as the bright light softened into a light glow, she was filled with love.

It was her Thammi!

Up and Down
OLIVER JEFFERS

"My dearest Shonamona," Thammi exclaimed, pulling her into a tight hug. "I have missed you so much. You are a big girl now and are soon going to start at a new school. Will you still play a little with your Thammi?"

"Thammi, you have come back!" Devika's voice was barely more than a whisper. "I never left you, my love," Thammi said softly. "When you need me, I will be here. To play with you. To talk to you. To do anything you like. What would you like to do?"

Devika did not have to think for long. "Let's read, read, read!" she declared and danced around her grandmother in excitement. Her Thammi laughed and spun her around in a circle. Then, Devika pulled out a stack of books and settled down on her Thammi's lap to read.

But what was this? As Thammi read from the books, the characters jumped off the pages and hopped around Devika. A black cat with white patches nestled up to her. A patchwork elephant began painting the walls with a brush. A lion preened in front of a bookshelf. A cat in a hat strolled across the room.

After a while, Thammi said it was time for her to go, she would return again tomorrow.

On Saturday morning, when Devika ran to her room, Thammi was already there. She was waiting for Devika with a bear puppet fitted on one hand and a dinosaur puppet on the other. She shot one arm towards her and the dinosaur roared. Devika giggled and jumped back.

"Have you ever done a puppet show inside a fort, my Shona?" Thammi asked her. Devika shook her head, feeling excitement bubble inside her. Thammi raised her palm towards the bookshelves. Devika watched in amazement as books floated out of shelves and arranged themselves on the floor in the shape of a giant fort.

Thammi ducked into the fort and beckoned to Devika to join her. She had laid out a long cloth with mirror work on it on the floor. They huddled in the cosy cave, surrounded by books. Thammi told her stories with puppets, figurines and masks. Sometimes, the puppets and figurines told the stories, while Thammi and Devika watched, enthralled.

By the time Devika felt hunger pangs for breakfast, Thammi had hugged her goodbye and whispered that she had something very special planned for them the next day.

Early on Sunday morning,
Devika snuck out of bed when it was still dark,
without waking her family. Entering her room, she saw
Thammi sitting on the windowsill, her legs dangling outside.

"Ah, my little Kuchipoo!" she beamed when she saw Devika. "Hop on, hop on!" When Devika reached her, she hoisted her up and swung her out of the window. "Hold tight, my love!" Thammi said as she wrapped her arms around Devika. Golden light started to whirl around them and Devika gasped as they began to spin. Before she knew it, they had shot into the sky amongst the stars!

"Where are we going, Thammi?" Devika asked her breathlessly.
"To the greatest library I have ever created, my love," Thammi told her.
"The greatest library in the galaxy. To the moon!"

Am I dreaming? Devika wondered as she clung to her Thammi, feeling wind and clouds whip past her and watching the moon grow closer and larger. They landed on its white surface. Before them was a large white dome with a small purple door. Thammi grasped Devika's hand and walked her through the door.

Devika's eyes grew large when she saw what was inside. It was a large room with multiple levels, each level full to the ceiling with books. Small creatures that Thammi told her were "Moonlittles" were choosing books, climbing ladders to reach the topmost shelves. A group of Moonlittles was sitting in front of a man with large spectacles in the centre. The man was reading to them. Others were lying on colourful cushions and in cosy nooks with books. Devika noticed a cave that Thammi told her would be filled with the perfect books for any child who entered it.

Thammi and Devika explored every corner of the most amazing library in the galaxy. "Thammi, can I come here everyday?" Devika asked her in a hushed voice after a while. Then, she remembered that her new school was beginning the next day. She felt tears spring into her eyes and clutched her Thammi's leg.

"What is worrying you, my love?" her Thammi asked her, stroking her head.

"I won't know anyone at my new school," Devika said with a sob. "What if I get lost? What if there are monsters there? What if I fall down? What if my new teacher does not understand what I am saying? I want to stay at home with Mamma and Daddy. I miss the teacher in my old school. I miss my friends. I want to read books with you and come to this library with you." Thammi drew her into a hug.

"Starting anything new can be scary," she said, "but, if you do it step by step, it won't be as scary as it seems right now. And whenever you need me again, I will come."

"Do you know, sweetheart," she continued. "I created the library in your new school. The librarian there is my friend. Say hello to her from me. She must be as nervous as you about all the new children coming to her library. Help her out, my little librarian."

This piqued Devika's interest. "I will practice in my library at home," she said thoughtfully.

At that, Thammi took Devika back home in a whirl of golden light.

Devika told her parents all about the Moon Library over breakfast.

ka loved to paint. She felt a little lighter. "I will paint a present for my sister!"
aid, a smile creeping onto her face.

, Devika was busy painting, building, mixing, singing, gardening, swinging.
etimes, she would remember her old school and her old friends. She thought
er parents and her little sister at home, doing the things they did every day.
would feel a lump form in her throat. But then she would spot something
resting and choose to focus on that instead. Step by step. After some time,
ika's teacher told the class that it was time to go to the library. Devika's heart
ped. The library! Thammi's library!

Then, she ran to her room and arranged all her toys like the Moonlittles she had seen gathered around the storyteller in the amphitheatre. She went through her bookshelves carefully, choosing the perfect book for each and every reader.

The next day, Devika dressed thoughtfully for school. She ate her pancake, put one small pony into her school bag and climbed into her car seat. When she felt panic rising inside her, she thought about her Thammi's words. Step by step.

When she reached the school gate, she clutched her Mamma's hand and shook her head. "I want to go to the moon with Thammi," she whispered, so softly that nobody could hear her. Mamma and Daddy told her they would be waiting for her here in just a few hours.

Devika's teacher was waiting at the gate to greet the children. She smiled at Devika and held out her hand.

"Come with me, my dear," she said. "Let me show you your classroom. Do you know, we are going to be painting today."

They were led through a bright purple door. Like the Moon Library, Devika thought to herself. On the other side of it was a room filled with books. Devika knew this room! She had seen pictures of it in Thammi's photo albums.

"Welcome, my new readers!" a lady called from the amphitheatre. "I am Ms Varma. Come, listen to a story!" She held up a book. It had a picture of a dog on it. Devika knew this book! It was about a detective dog and a book thief. "Now, tell me, how many of you have a dog at home?" Devika's hand shot up, along with a few others. "Ah! We must invite them all to the library one day," Ms Varma smiled.

Ms Varma began to read the story and the children listened with rapt attention. When the story was over, Ms Varma showed them where they could find books for themselves. "You can look at them on your own or ask any of us to read to you or issue any three to take home with you."

As the other children spread out to look at the books and toys around them, Devika approached Ms Varma and asked her about her Thammi.

Then, she ran to her room and arranged all her toys like the Moonlittles she had seen gathered around the storyteller in the amphitheatre. She went through her bookshelves carefully, choosing the perfect book for each and every reader.

The next day, Devika dressed thoughtfully for school. She ate her pancake, put one small pony into her school bag and climbed into her car seat. When she felt panic rising inside her, she thought about her Thammi's words. Step by step.

When she reached the school gate, she clutched her Mamma's hand and shook her head. "I want to go to the moon with Thammi," she whispered, so softly that nobody could hear her. Mamma and Daddy told her they would be waiting for her here in just a few hours.

Devika's teacher was waiting at the gate to greet the children. She smiled at Devika and held out her hand.

"Come with me, my dear," she said. "Let me show you your classroom. Do you know, we are going to be painting today."

Devika loved to paint. She felt a little lighter. "I will paint a present for my sister!" she said, a smile creeping onto her face.

Soon, Devika was busy painting, building, mixing, singing, gardening, swinging. Sometimes, she would remember her old school and her old friends. She thought of her parents and her little sister at home, doing the things they did every day. She would feel a lump form in her throat. But then she would spot something interesting and choose to focus on that instead. Step by step. After some time, Devika's teacher told the class that it was time to go to the library. Devika's heart jumped. The library! Thammi's library!

They were led through a bright purple door. Like the Moon Library, Devika thought to herself. On the other side of it was a room filled with books. Devika knew this room! She had seen pictures of it in Thammi's photo albums.

“Welcome, my new readers!” a lady called from the amphitheatre. “I am Ms Varma. Come, listen to a story!” She held up a book. It had a picture of a dog on it. Devika knew this book! It was about a detective dog and a book thief. “Now, tell me, how many of you have a dog at home?” Devika’s hand shot up, along with a few others. “Ah! We must invite them all to the library one day,” Ms Varma smiled.

Ms Varma began to read the story and the children listened with rapt attention. When the story was over, Ms Varma showed them where they could find books for themselves. “You can look at them on your own or ask any of us to read to you or issue any three to take home with you.”

As the other children spread out to look at the books and toys around them, Devika approached Ms Varma and asked her about her Thammi.

The Detective Dog
Mom

"Ms Sen!" Ms Varma exclaimed, enveloping Devika in a hug. "Ms Sen was my most favourite person in the whole world. She created this library. Do you know what she used to say to me, Devika? She said, 'At any given moment, for every child, there is a perfect book and, for every book, there is a perfect child. It is our job to make the two meet each other'."

Devika felt suddenly sad, thinking about her Thammi and about the 'Find Your Perfect Book Cave' in the Moon Library. Ms Varma was still crouching before her. She looked deep into Devika's eyes and took one of Devika's hands in hers. "Devika, will you be my assistant and help me find the perfect book for each one of your friends?"

Devika nodded with delight. Ms Varma and she wove their way through all the children and books. Ms Varma handed Devika some books and told her to ask her friends to choose from those options.

When library time was over, Ms Varma whispered to Devika, "I will see you again tomorrow, my little librarian!"

When Devika returned home that day, she told her parents all about her new school, Thammi's library and Thammi's friend.

"She told me I could be her assistant," Devika told them, before vanishing into her room to set up her pretend library again. "I am the librarian," she told her little sister. "You be my assistant."

At bedtime, Daddy read her the three books she had issued from the school library, plus a few more from the home library. Devika held up one that Ms Varma had recommended to her about a magician who visited a library and pulled out books from a magical hat. "Daddy, this was the perfect book for me today," she said.

Daddy smiled and asked, "Does this mean we will be reading it again tomorrow?" Devika shrugged sleepily, her eyes still closed. "A different book will be perfect tomorrow. I will find it in my library."

"The school library or the home library?" Daddy asked. "Or the Moon Library?" he murmured. But Devika was already asleep.

Kafka
ZAKIR and his tabla
Dha Dhin Na

About Bandana Sen

My mother-in-law, Bandana Sen (14.09.1943 - 01.06.2018), was a pioneer in the field of children's libraries and reading programs in India. When my husband and I were pregnant with our first daughter, she did indeed decide to sidestep the usual, practical grandparent gifts and present her grandchild with a physical manifestation of her life's work – a library of her own.

Born and raised in Darjeeling, West Bengal, Thammi began her career working at the American International School in Calcutta. She spent close to four decades managing libraries at the American Embassy School in New Delhi and then another 12 years setting up libraries at Pathways Schools across NCR.

A thought leader in her field, my mother-in-law believed the library to be the sanctum of any educational institution and a vibrant reading culture essential to any society. She saw reading as a unifying force for children and a medium through which all of life's values could be taught. She felt that children need to read or be read to every single day. Her ethos was to make children active participants in their learning by offering them vast quantities of books on every subject, laid out in an inviting manner, and allowing them to lead their own reading journey. With her own vibrant, creative and sparkling personality, she made reading fun.

During her lifetime, Thammi helped create world-class libraries and reading programs across the country, nurtured a love for reading in thousands of children and mentored an entire generation of librarians to carry on her work. She felt strongly that librarians should be thoroughly familiar with the books in their libraries and make a genuine effort to get to know children intimately so that they could guide them in an authentic manner. She saw every library as uniquely reflecting the personality and perspective of the librarians who created it.

Outspoken and unorthodox, she had an amazing zest for life and a love of all things beautiful. She had a museum-quality collection of silver jewellery and an almost academically curated selection of saris. She wore a signature chunky necklace and stately armband every day. The fact that she was an incurable aesthete manifested itself best in her drawing room, which was as much a canvas for her as her libraries were. Every inch of wall space was covered in paintings. Her floor-level furniture was adorned with beautiful textiles and artefacts she had acquired on her extensive travels.

It was this hunger for beauty and new experiences that made her the talented librarian she was. Her libraries were not simply reading spaces, they were cultural spaces. She saw books as cultural artefacts that had to be understood in a larger context. She wanted her students to use books to become thinking individuals but also to love books because they cherished and understood the beauty of all things.

Her loss in 2018 had been sudden and unexpected. It left my husband, Akash, and me shattered, unable to understand how our two-and-a-half-year-old and four-month-old daughters got such little time with someone who loved them so dearly. One of the starkest reminders of our bereavement was the library in our nursery – a vast and gorgeous collection that was actually larger than anything I could have dreamed of on my own. Over fifteen hundred books spread across bookshelves that covered more than half our wall space spilled into every available crevice in the room, but we knew that it was incomplete. She had so much left to give us, so much work left to do. At the same time, it was the most precious inheritance she could have left her granddaughters.

- Himani Dalmia

Acknowledgements

The idea for this book germinated from an article I wrote on our home library for Scroll.in's Publishing and the Pandemic series. I'm indebted to my dear friend, Neha Bhatt, who suggested the article to me and showed me the story hidden in our stories. The series was the brainchild of Kanishka Gupta, also my agent. I'm grateful to him for motivating me to write the piece and then the book.

Tina Narang at HarperCollins India, who believed in the book from day one, and Priya Kuriyan, many of whose books already lined the shelves of our home library, brought this book to life and took a very personal story to the world at large. It was a pleasure to work with them.

My daughters, Devika and Yamini, showed me the brilliance of children's books with their unadulterated delight in them from day one. Seeing through their eyes revealed the magic to me and I'm smitten for life. I see their Thammi in their faces every day and she would have been so proud of the little thinkers and doers they are growing into.

And, finally, the deepest love and gratitude for my husband, Akash Premsen, who far surpasses any image of husband, father and son that I could ever dream up.

Himani Dalmia is mamma to two little read-o-sauruses, Devika and Yamini, in addition to three dogs and several fish. When she isn't reading to all of them, she is cooking up stories on her laptop or helping little ones sleep better as a baby and toddler sleep specialist. She is the author of *Life is Perfect*, a novel for adults, and co-author of *Sleeping Like a Baby: the Art & Science of Gentle Baby Sleep*, a bedside companion for parents of 0-5 year olds. She is co-founder of the large parenting community, *Gentle Baby Sleep India*, and a leader of the *La Leche League*. She earned a Master's in South Asian Literature from the University of Oxford after graduating with honours in English from St. Stephen's College, Delhi University. Married to her high school sweetheart, Akash Premsen, Himani had a front-row seat to her super cool mother-in-law Bandana Sen's work in the field of children's libraries for two decades. As a parent counsellor, Himani is a staunch advocate of the power of children's literature to inspire, inform, heal and nourish.

Priya Kuriyan is a children's book writer-illustrator and comics maker. She has directed educational films for the *Sesame Street show* (India) and the *Children's Film Society of India* (CFSI) and has illustrated numerous children's books for publishers like *Tulika Books*, *Karadi Tales*, *Eklavya, HarperCollins, Scholastic and Penguin books*. Her work has appeared in publications like the *Mint Lounge, The Indian Express, The Indian Quarterly* and *The Hindu Business Line*. In 2019, she won the 'Big Little Book Award', instituted by Parag, an initiative of Tata Trusts to recognize her contribution to children's literature in India. She lives and works in the city of Bangalore, and in her spare time likes to make funny caricatures of its residents.